RESPONSIBILITY CENTER MANAGEMENT

Lessons from 25 Years
of Decentralized Management

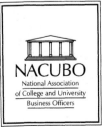

NACUBO
National Association
of College and University
Business Officers

Jon C. Strauss

John R. Curry

Responsibility Center Management: 25 Years of Lessons Learned
is made possible by a generous grant from
PRAGER, MCCARTHY & SEALY, LLC

National Association of College and University Business Officers
Washington, DC
www.nacubo.org

Printed in the United States of America

ISBN 1-56972-020-7

Contents

Acknowledgements iv

Preface v

    Table 1 vii

Chapter 1: Introduction 1

Chapter 2: Principles 7

Chapter 3: Budgeting and Planning...................................... 9

Chapter 4: Guidelines... 11

Chapter 5: Details 13

Chapter 6: Answering the Critics.. 15

Chapter 7: Promise and Performance.................................. 23

Chapter 8: Lessons Learned 33

Chapter 9: Conclusions 37

Bibliography 39

Acknowledgements

The authors would like to acknowledge the insights provided by the following individuals:

University of Pennsylvania
    Eduardo Glandt, dean, School of Engineering and Applied Science
    Michael Masch, executive director, Office of Budget and
        Management Analysis
    Samuel H. Preston, dean, School of Arts and Sciences
    Peter Traber, CEO, University of Pennsylvania Medical Center
    and Health System

University of Southern California
    Lloyd Armstrong Jr., provost and senior vice president
        for academic affairs
    Scott H. Bice, dean emeritus of the Law School
    Dennis F. Dougherty, senior vice president for administration

Indiana University
    Maynard Thompson, vice-chancellor/dean, budgetary
        administration and planning
    Judith G. Palmer, vice president and chief financial officer

Claremont Graduate University
    Steadman Upham, president

Kaludis Consulting Group
    Glen Stine, vice president

University of Denver
    Craig Woody, vice-chancellor for financial affairs/treasurer

NACUBO is grateful to Prager, McCarthy & Sealy, LLC for contributing to the publication costs of this volume.

Preface

Decentralization is a natural act in universities. Decentralization of authority, that is. Decentralization of responsibility is not a natural act. That requires intention and design. Many academic leaders will say that most authority lies with the faculty in departments and schools, and most responsibility lies with central administrators. In many universities today, this state still obtains yet is more often lamented than addressed and managed. Increasing numbers of institutions, however, are making explicit efforts to address such imbalances, to design organizational structures and incentives to make responsibility commensurate with authority, wherever that authority lies.

The problem we address is the decoupling of academic authority from financial responsibility. The solution we propose for the coupling is Responsibility Center Management (RCM), also called Revenue Responsibility Budgeting (RRB).

Examples of decoupling abound. Faculty make decisions within departments about curriculum, admissions requirements, class size, and numbers of sections offered. Such decisions affect the number of admissible freshmen, access to popular majors, and time until degree. These, in turn, can have major impacts on enrollments, and hence tuition revenues. Yet such decisions are all too often uninformed by their financial consequences. Revenues are someone else's problem: the provost's, the admissions director's, or the chief financial officer's; that is, the people responsible for revenues. Faculty members may apply for and win a research award with implications for additional laboratory space and admission of more graduate students to support the research agenda—both with financial consequences for central administrators responsible for space allocation, renovation, and construction—that is, for the facilities' indirect costs supporting research. But that's someone else's problem, too!

Responsibility Center Management attempts to couple such decisions with their consequences by making a fundamental trade: ownership of revenues for financial responsibility, including the indirect costs of programs. Thus, for example, a school of engineering in a large university would own, or keep, tuition revenues generated by engineering class enrollments, and research revenue (including indirect cost recovery) generated by engineering faculty principal investigators. In exchange, the school would budget expenses (including indirect costs) within its revenue envelope, and actively manage revenue ups and downs. Tuition up, hire faculty and add new course sections; tuition down, scale back recruitment and reduce sections and numbers of teaching assistants. Research volume (revenues) up, plan for new space and use incremental indirect cost recovery to pay interest on financing and to cover depreciation and operations. Research volume down, yield space to other academic departments with revenues available to cover the costs. In both these examples, choice and consequence are coupled.

By way of early introduction, Table 1 illustrates a prototypical responsibility center budget format for a university with two schools, A and B, and a central administration. In particular, the table shows each school's ownership of revenues and indirect expenses. It also introduces the concepts of participation and subvention, about which more follows. John Curry has presented a succinct introduction to this subject matter (J. R. Curry, 2000).

Starting with Harvard's *Each Tub on its Own Bottom* and moving forward in time to the University of Pennsylvania's *Responsibility Center Management*, the University of Southern California's *Revenue Center Management*, and Indiana University's *Responsibility Center Budgeting*, a rich history of the design and use of formal decentralized management systems in higher education is evolving. We have been part of that history. Jon Strauss was chief budget officer at Penn during the implementation of Responsibility Center Management, chief administrative officer at USC during the implementation of Revenue Center Management, and president of Worcester Polytechnic Institute during their experiments with decentralized management. John Curry was chief budget officer at USC during their implementation of Revenue Center Management, chief administrative officer at UCLA during their experiments with de-centralized management, and consultant to Indiana during the development of Responsibility Center Budgeting.

Having been part of this, we are curious to see what history has taught us. In this monograph we will: review some of the highlights of formal (or designed) decentralized management systems (using RCM as the rubric); explore the fundamental principles and guidelines of such systems; contrast the promise

TABLE 1

RESPONSIBILITY CENTER BUDGET FORMAT (in $000,000)
PROTOTYPICAL UNIVERSITY

	Administration Centers	Academic Centers		Total
		School A	School B	
DIRECT REVENUES				
Tuition	0	120	60	180
Financial Aid	0	(20)	(10)	(30)
Endowment & Gifts				
Unrestricted	40	0	0	40
Restricted	0	30	50	80
Research				
Restricted	0	100	200	300
F&A Recovery	0	60	120	180
INDIRECT REVENUES				
Participation @20% of unrestricted revenues	66	(32)	(34)	0
Subvention	(106)	42	64	0
Total Revenues	**0**	**300**	**450**	**750**
DIRECT EXPENDITURES				
Instruction	0	100	100	200
Research	0	100	200	300
Facilities	150	0	0	150
Administration	100	0	0	100
INDIRECT EXPENDITURES				
Facilities	(150)	60	90	0
Administration	(100)	40	60	0
Total Expenditures	**0**	**300**	**450**	**750**

of these systems with performance; evaluate many of the common criticisms; and report on the experiences of several institutions that have developed and refined decentralization methodologies. Our perspectives come from some 25 years of experience in pioneering new approaches to the effective management of complex universities. Moreover, our assessments and commentary have gained currency from recent visits to the Universities of Pennsylvania and Southern California, the self-assessment of Indiana University, Bloomington, (N. Theobald and M. Thompson, 2000), and observations from a number of reviewers and participants in several decentralized systems.

And so, we have a simple goal in this brief monograph: to answer the question, "How is responsibility center management working?" Is it the work of deities or the work of the devil? It has always amazed us just how many fundamental academic questions get tangled up in Table 1 when the numbers begin to change and ownership of the increments is at stake.

Chapter 1

Introduction

Few enterprises in our society are more innately decentralized than colleges and universities. The traditions of collegial governance are deep rooted, the school/department/program structure being almost universal. The faculty have authority over hires, fires, marketing, production, quality control, and most expenditures. By virtue of tenure, they have a strong vesting in the success of the institution, but typically as seen from a departmental perspective. Faculty, with all their authority and independence, however, do not always exercise appropriate responsibility to their institutions. Indeed, what is best for institutions as a whole may not be the sum of individual departmental optima.

In his essay on these issues, Alan Wolfe (A. Wolfe, 1996) suggests that one consequence of this natural decentralization is that: "…the university is not an entity with a common purpose, or at least organized around a system-defining core." He then goes on to claim this decentralization in combination with the institution of tenure: "…explains the failures of faculty self governance." We have a different take, namely that decentralized authority and competing, sometimes inconsistent goals—indeed, the lack of a "system-defining core"—are in the very nature of universities. They are realities to be reckoned with rather than pathologies to be lamented. Further, reformulating and formalizing this natural decentralization in the management structure and incentives of the institution can not only mitigate the decoupling of responsibility from authority, but also accentuate the positive attributes of decentralization.

The fundamental premise of RCM is the completion of the authority-responsibility circle within affinity groups of disciplines: giving the faculty of schools or departments specific, measurable incentives to exercise their considerable authority *responsibly* for the benefit of themselves, their students, their organizational units, and the institution as a whole. With the right incentives, faculty become advocates for change and actions they might normally resist strongly if advocated by others, especially central administrators.

Experiences at Penn (L.B. Salamon and J.C. Strauss, 1979), USC (J.R. Curry, 1996), and Indiana University (E.L. Whalen, 1991; N. Theobald and M. Thompson, 2000), indicate that financial incentives can be tailored to encourage alignment with the institutional goals. Take, for example, the goals of improving undergraduate teaching and timely progress to degree. When tuition revenues are allocated to the courses where students enroll, it is easy to see that the major source of revenue (especially net revenue—after costs) for most schools and programs is undergraduate enrollment, and the best way to increase that revenue is by offering courses students need and improving the quality of teaching. And, by increasing revenue, faculty achieve greater latitude to increase numbers of colleagues, improve working conditions, and even increase compensation, thereby connecting self and institutional interests. There is increasing recognition in the higher education literature (R. Zemsky, 1993; J.R. Curry, 1996) of the importance of financial incentives, particularly as applied to budgeting and planning, in this regard.

Martin Meyerson, president of the University of Pennsylvania in the early 1970s, championed the development of Responsibility Center Management (L.B. Salamon and J.C. Strauss, 1979). By bringing marketplace incentives to higher education, he hoped to involve faculty and others in considering financial as well as academic issues when making trade-offs between competing claims for limited resources. Before, and to this day at many colleges and universities, most faculty consider only academic issues in budget and space allocation decision processes and then resist administrative concerns for financial viability. They engage in local benefit analysis—cost and revenue analysis are missing. Meyerson's insight into the effectiveness of decentralized management at both improving decisions and reducing administrator/faculty conflict proved prescient. And, while this new approach did not automate management or eliminate the need for difficult decisions, it helped create a climate where decisions could be made within the appropriate context, more rapidly, and with potentially greater collegiality.

Subsequently, during our simultaneous tenures as administrators at USC in the early 1980s, we worked with Provost C. J. Pings to develop a similar approach to decentralized management, called Revenue Center Management (J.R. Curry, 1996) to ratify and rationalize local revenue hunting and gathering, as well as to emphasize the importance of revenue development in the decentralized units in general. Then, in the late 1980s, Tom Erlich, formerly provost at Penn and then president of Indiana University, brought Responsibility Center Budgeting (E.L. Whalen, 1991), since renamed Responsibility Centered Management (N. Theobald and M. Thompson, 2000), to the public sector. Still later, there has been vigorous activity in formalizing decentralized management at such disparate independent institutions as Claremont Graduate University (CGU), Rensselaer Polytechnic Institute, the University of Denver, and Vanderbilt; and public universities such as Illinois, Michigan, Minnesota, and UCLA. Whatever the name, RCM has taken root in a variety of colleges and universities and, we believe, been proven effective in both private and public settings against its original objectives: clarifying roles and responsibilities between local and central units, linking cause and effect through revenue and indirect cost allocations, placing local academic planning and decision making in a cost/benefit context, and unleashing entrepreneurship. RCM has given rise to other problems, however, which we address later.

As typically implemented, RCM prescribes revenue and indirect cost allocation (ownership) rules and then gives schools and other revenue-generating units the responsibility to cover the total costs of their programs—indirect, as well as direct—from the revenues generated by their teaching, research, or business service activities. Program revenues include tuition, gifts, endowment, research and service income, and indirect cost recoveries. In addition, most successful RCM implementations collect general institutional revenues and then allocate them differentially and discriminately to the various units as *subvention*. The "subvention pool" may also be funded from school-specific revenue taxes, sometimes euphemistically called *participation*.

By explicitly allocating the costs of facilities and administrative services to the revenue producing centers, RCM provides information on full program costs while encouraging attention to the quality and efficient production of these services. Indeed, if centers have to use *their* revenues to pay for these services, they should use cost information to challenge the purveyors (vendors). Early experience at both Penn and USC (J.C. Strauss, 1985) suggested that this attention could lead to both reduction in costs and improvement in service quality. But, recent conversations with both institutions confirm that continual scrutiny is required to maintain efficiency. Left to their own devices, even academic administrators tend to forget that their administrative services exist to support the academic mission, not to support self-defined ends.

The development, protection, and wise use of centrally earned revenues—the filling and care of the subvention pool—are important to the financial and academic success of RCM. Sources of funding for subvention typically include unrestricted endowment and investment income, unrestricted gifts, or general state appropriations. Since RCM works best when all centers are dependent on at least some subvention—independent programs are integrated in part by a common need for subvention—most universities have imposed revenue taxes to enlarge the subvention pool. For example, Penn has a 20 percent "University Tuition" and USC a 20 percent "Participation" on all unrestricted center-owned revenues. Such taxes explicitly recognize the fact that students and research dollars are attracted to both the institution and the individual responsibility centers.

With subventions, presidents and provosts can compensate for the wide disparities in unit costs of different academic programs of equivalent quality (contrast business and engineering, for example) that typically charge the same tuition unit price, or receive the same per-student state support. More important, though, are incentives which reward the development and execution of sound academic plans with allocations of subvention in proportion to plan success and consonance with the mission of the institution. This issue of forging and holding the center—assuring achievement of institutional as well as local goals, thus making the whole greater than the sum of the parts—is a core concern about RCM, about which more follows. Still a third use of subventions is provision of start-up funds for promising new academic ventures. It is crucial that the allocation of these funds (as subventions) not be prescribed by formula. While some argue that subvention is an arcane art, subjective discretion is absolutely essential lest subventions become hardened and irretrievable.

Acknowledging and being open about internal resource reallocations is important to the integrity of RCM. For example, Johns Hopkins suffered a well-publicized failure of decentralized management some years ago principally because the university had no formal mechanism to reallocate funds to support their high quality, but expensive, arts and sciences programs. Interschool subsidies were implicit, buried in year-end consolidated financial statements, rather than openly understood as integral to their system. On the other hand, Harvard's infamous ETOB system—each tub on its own bottom—has functioned very well for many years with each school totally responsible for its own finances and with no inter-school reallocation mechanisms. Part of

Harvard's success is due to having all undergraduate programs within one school, part is due to having an abundance of resources, and part no doubt is due to Harvard being Harvard. Those close to the Harvard scene, however, report a significant level of inter-school contention and enormous difficulty in reaching agreement on common services, to say nothing of common directions and synergies between tubs. In fact, Nannerl Keohane, president of Duke University, commented recently in the *Harvard Magazine* (N.O. Keohane, 2001) that: "Having each tub on its own bottom ... may not be an advantage when the whole enterprise needs to head briskly in some new direction."

Glen Stine, former budget director at both Penn and the University of Colorado, notes that operating budget dollars are not the only sources of "subvention" to help encourage on-mission behavior from the centers. Other important centrally dispensed incentives include capital, access to debt, access to donors, and priority positions in fund-raising campaigns.

We also note that RCM is well-aligned with the burgeoning assessment movement, wherein accountability is measured by outcomes rather than controlled by inputs. In RCM, schools and other responsibility centers are accountable for both academic and financial performance. Good academic performance vis-à-vis plans can be reinforced with additional subvention. Financial shortfalls are carried forward, to be repaid from future year resources, and surpluses are saved and invested for new endeavors, or protection against future deficits. And, the administrative centers are encouraged to provide competitive quality services consistent with their costs, which are charged to the revenue-producing centers. Accountability is further advanced in that, typically, academic and financial "bottom lines" are made public.

Chapter 2

Principles

In the early 1980s, the committee appointed to develop what became Revenue Center Management at USC enunciated a set of broad organizational principles to guide their deliberations, and ultimately to shape the new system. In Chapter 7 of *Resource Allocation in Higher Education* (Curry, 1996), John Curry describes these principles:

1. The closer the decisionmaker is to the relevant information, the better the decision is likely to be. (If you are too far removed from the action, you don't know enough to make a decision, and even if you do, you are too remote to implement it.)

2. The degree of decentralization of an organization should be proportional to its size and complexity. (Management scope should be limited to what you can do.)

3. Responsibility should be commensurate with authority and vice versa. (Those who have the power to act should know the consequences and be responsible for them.)

4. The central administration should retain sufficient academic and fiscal leverage to ensure achievement of institutional goals. (Local optimization does not always lead to globally optimal outcomes.)

5. Clear rewards and sanctions are required to make the distribution of responsibility and authority operational, as well as to effect their coupling. (If no one wins or loses when things go right or wrong, no one is responsible.)

6. Resource-expanding incentives are preferable to resource-dividing rules. (Entrepreneurs are more fun than tax lawyers.)

7. Successful decentralization requires common information systems providing local and central managers with timely and accurate performance reports. (Dueling data dilute responsibility.)

8. Outcome measures are preferable to input (process) controls. (Delivery is *the* goal.)

9. Achievement of academic excellence requires that academic performance criteria be explicit and, where possible, quantified (lest financial currency drive out academic currency, a form of Gresham's Law.)

10. Stable financial environments facilitate good planning. (Rapid fluctuations in resources play havoc with education and research.)

11. People play better games when they own the rules.

These principles will come into play later on as we assess the criticisms, promise, practice, and refinements of RCM.

Chapter 3

Budgeting and Planning

At the core of RCM is prospective budgeting and planning. The typical approach to developing the annual budget in RCM from the central budget officer's vantage point is this:

1. Project the full institutional budget for the next year(s) and make preliminary trade-offs among tuition rates, enrollments, salaries, benefits, new programs, changes in administrative services, and the academic/administrative balance of any required expenditure reductions.

2. Estimate preliminary budgets for the administrative service centers based on the overall budget situation and the required quality and amount of specific services.

3. Use these preliminary administrative service center budgets to allocate preliminary indirect costs for the next year to the revenue centers based on established algorithms using the relative size and usage data from the prior and current year.

4. Project tuition revenues and financial aid for the next year based on the new provisional rates and the expected enrollments.

5. Set preliminary subventions for the revenue centers (e.g., colleges, schools) to reflect unit price/cost balance, priority, and changes required to achieve the goals of the strategic plan.

6. Within these preliminary guidelines, charge the responsibility centers to balance their budgets, with particular care for the assumptions regarding revenues and the justification of deviations from initial conditions: enrollment changes, research volume changes, proposals for differential tuition prices or salary increases, among other deviations. Similarly, charge administrative centers to propose "appropriately constrained" budgets.

7. Allow for structured review and feedback with respect to preliminary subvention and administrative service allocations, and proposed deviations from initial guidelines.

8. Rebalance the whole by vetting and refining the revenue and service centers' proposed budgets.

Table 1 (page vii) exhibits a Responsibility Center Management budget balanced across centers (School A, School B and Central Administration) among the constituent parts: local revenues, central revenues, direct and indirect costs, and subvention.

Once this logic is in place, various refinements can be added to do planning and subvention settings over longer time periods. Institutions also need a mechanism, perhaps an *inter-center bank*, to account for surpluses and deficits, both to pay interest on and plan withdrawals from surpluses (deposits), and to charge interest on and schedule repayments of deficits (loans).

As with all budgeting, it is important to view the developing annual budget as the next year of the rolling implementation of a longer-term strategic plan. RCM facilitates this view by involving more than the usual number of constituencies in the process of planning and validating the revenue assumptions and making the necessary expense trade-offs. Moreover, RCM requires explicit and public reallocation of resources between and among the various centers. In the absence of a generally agreed upon plan, such reallocations can be difficult to explain and defend.

Chapter 4

Guidelines

Our conversations with leaders, as well as our own experiences at Penn, USC, UCLA, and Indiana in implementing and managing decentralized management and budgeting systems, suggest several guidelines, many based on the principles above.

- Keep it simple! Folks will argue both sides of any algorithm to distribute revenues or allocate costs. There is no perfect algorithm.

- Develop broad-based involvement and acceptance for the underlying principles early on. They will guide intelligent evolution of the system.

- Test proposed allocation rule changes against the principles.

- Maintain as much discretion as possible in the allocation of central resources (subvention).

- Derive all reports directly from official information systems used by all units and make certain that reports reconcile. One simple mistake or inconsistency can destroy confidence for a long time.

- Emphasize that while numbers reconcile to the official information systems, the underlying decisions reflect academic priorities and judgments.

- Display and budget all financial activities—sources and uses—to emphasize their role in advancing the missions of the academic units.

- Avoid the temptation to deal solely with the direct revenues and expenses as this precludes the benefits of knowing the overheads no matter how imprecisely they are allocated. (Estimating the indirect cost implications of decisions and sustaining revenue center back pressure on service costs and quality are essential to system efficacy.)

- Never (ever!) compromise the principle that units must be responsible for their financial, as well as their academic performance. Provostial forgiveness of decanal deficits constitutes what economists call moral hazard.

- Embed the annual budgeting process in a multi-year strategic planning process.

- Present all data (except individual salaries) for all units publicly to encourage comparison, publicize priorities, and reduce suspicion.

- Constantly emphasize and demonstrate that RCM is a means to academic ends. Make the ends drive the means (lest financial conversations drive out academic ones).

- The president and chief academic officer (and trustees) must believe in the process (i.e., walk it as well as talk it)!

We will reprise several of these later, but against a richer contextual backdrop, in "Lessons Learned."

Chapter 5

Details

For readers interested in the details behind a prototypical responsibility center budget, we return to Table 1 (page vii) where we focus on Schools A and B. Here are some prototypical algorithms governing A's and B's revenue and indirect cost allocations by line item:

Tuition: We will suppose that tuition revenues are allocated in proportion to credit hours taught. Thus School A generates 67 percent of total credit hours (100/150) and School B, 33 percent (50/150). An alternative algorithm might recognize that the majoring school should receive some direct portion of tuition revenues to represent the fact that it attracted the student's interest (and tuition payments) and incurs advising costs. Thus one might allocate 80 percent of total tuition revenues in proportion to credit hours generated, and 20 percent in proportion to total numbers of majors.

Institutional financial *aid* would typically be allocated in proportion to tuition revenues, in recognition that aid policy is set by the institution rather than the centers. In some cases, however, we have seen aid summed across students in individual courses, with the net revenues allocated to the course and hence to the teaching center. (This penalizes schools that attract and teach needy students, and is accounting overkill in our view.) In accordance with accounting principles, aid would be subtracted from gross tuition. Table 1 shows $30 million in financial aid distributed to centers A and B in the same ratio as their tuition revenues.

Endowment & Gifts: Unrestricted endowments and gifts belong to the central administration and fill subvention pool. Restricted gifts belong to the centers A and B.

Research: Direct research expenditures are owned by faculty principal investigators in the individual schools A and B. Indirect cost recovery is allocated to the schools whose faculty members have the grants and contracts. Recoveries belong with the schools that incur, and are allocated, the indirect costs of doing research.

Participation is a charge of 20 percent of unrestricted center revenues available to fill the subvention pool. Table 1 exhibits the flow of participation from centers A and B into the administration center, where it is added to centrally owned endowment and gifts to form a subvention pool of $106 million.

Subvention is a discretionary allocation of general institutional revenues, including the proceeds from participation. Subvention allocations balance the impacts of different unit costs among diverse academic programs—historical, intrinsic, or desired—and fund institutional priorities. Looking at Table 1, we see a subvention pool of $106 million, with $42 million allocated to academic center A and $64 million to center B. We might infer that School B is higher in the priority pecking order, with its $64 million subvention, or that its unit costs are higher (perhaps because it is more research intensive and recovers indirect costs through an average rate), or both.

Indirect income is the sum of participation and subvention. For center A, this is $10 million, for B, $30 million. Some would argue that indirect income is a subsidy, and therefore B is more subsidized than A. This is a facile argument, valid only when administrative indirect cost allocations are "perfect" and unit costs match unit prices. We should beware of simple interpretations in RCM.

Indirect expenditures come in two varieties. *Facilities* comprise utilities, repair and maintenance, custodial service, interest on related debt, and depreciation (or a substitute like 2 percent of replacement costs). Utility metering and good occupancy and cost data allow very accurate allocation of facilities expenditures to responsibility centers.

Indirect *administrative* expenditures are another matter. Student services, for example, might be allocated in proportion to majors or credit hours generated in a center. Here one attempts to measure usage. With more centralized, less direct services, such as the controller's office, allocation is typically in proportion to total expenditures of a center. In Table 1, center A has direct expenditures of $200 million, B of $300 million. The administrative costs of $100 million are allocated in the same 2-to-3 ratio: $40 million to A, $60 million to B. Here the rule is based on access or potential use. A more extensive elaboration of indirect cost allocation methodologies is provided in Ed Whalen's book, *Responsibility Center Budgeting* (E.L. Whalen, 1991).

Chapter 6

Answering the Critics

Our recent visits to Penn and USC and review of Indiana's self-study (N. Theobald and M. Thompson, 2000) confirm that for every claimed or demonstrated success of RCM, there is a companion criticism. We attempt to evaluate criticisms.

- **Decisions are driven more by financial than academic considerations.**

  The problem with this criticism is that it is just as applicable to highly centralized budget structures as to RCM. Indeed, we have yet to see an academic consideration not ultimately tied to a financial one! The only question is the length of the tether! The promise of RCM is in joining academic and financial considerations together in the right place. Indeed, the difference between centralized systems and RCM is that finance quantifies the decisions and plans more locally and broadly in RCM, as there are more people with more perspectives involved to talk about it. Just as there is more criticism of institutional rankings by those ranked poorly, so too is this criticism more likely to come from those accorded lower priority for central funds (e.g., "my claims are academic, the dean's or provost's response is financial"). The simple facts of the matter are that academic values must drive, and be seen and heard to drive, the financial decisions expressed through relative subvention, and that resource availability will force priorities and thus drive academic choice.

  Leaders have to work to maintain balance. It is an intentional and irrefutable fact that "local" decisions under RCM require several more financial considerations than do decisions under decoupled centralized structures.

- **RCM raises barriers to cross-disciplinary programs between schools.**

That this concern for disincentives for cross-disciplinary work has been raised since the first days of RCM suggests a problem. We have noted elsewhere (see Curry in E.L. Whalen, 1991) that disciplinary barriers are already so high, that this criticism of RCM may be more prejudice than fact, and thus a new excuse for cold pursuit of cross-disciplinary programs. Regardless, Lloyd Armstrong, USC provost, reports success with using subvention to encourage interdisciplinary work, and the Indiana University Bloomington (IUB) RCM Review Committee (N. Theobald and M. Thompson, 2000) "finds the reality to be very different. By making costs and benefits much easier to quantify, RCM fosters cross-disciplinary, integrated projects across schools." IU has used the role of vice president or vice chancellor for research effectively in brokering explicit revenue and cost-sharing research pacts among departments and schools. So if the criticism is true, then there are clearly ways to lower the barriers.

- **Financial incentives encourage inappropriate faculty behavior.**

Some may be surprised to learn how little personal gain serves as an incentive for individual faculty performance. Most faculty are concerned that they benefit through their work and that of their colleagues. Once they are satisfied that their compensation reflects their contributions, relative to their peers, faculty appear to be more comfortable to quantify those "benefits" in disciplinary terms such as new colleagues, research lab upgrades, increased library and travel budgets, and more departmental staff support. RCM can help set specific incentives for faculty performance with appropriate rewards on both individual and disciplinary bases. And when incentives are explicit, and discovered to engender bad behavior, the incentives can be changed. When latent incentives encourage bad behavior—and they do—the problem is hard to diagnose and solve.

- **Tensions are exacerbated.**

There is no question that decentralized management makes public the relative financial performance and the relative priority as expressed through subvention of each of the centers. The system also encourages the revenue centers to bargain openly with service center providers. RCM's intent is making existing, typically longstanding, tensions more constructive, i.e., to focus the tensions on achieving the common good. While there is no denying such tension, it is refreshing when arguments are couched in a common RCM vocabulary and the analytic comparisons have a common standard. For example, knowing the cost per square foot for maintenance of her buildings, a dean can ask how this compares with outsourced services. Anecdotal complaints are converted to price/quality comparisons. IUB's RCM Review Committee (N. Theobald and M. Thompson, 2000) lauds other aspects of this tension in noting: "RCM creates a tension between the drive to uphold quality and to maintain student enrollments." Some tensions need to be exacerbated!

- **Schools can erect trade barriers.**

Enterprising, but misguided, centers can seek to retain their enrolled students' tuition by limiting students' abilities to take courses in other schools —a credit hour grab. Both Penn and USC cite examples of their engineering schools finding compelling arguments for their students to need courses in mathematics and communications taught by engineering faculty rather than arts and sciences faculty. Their management schools have been known to introduce special statistics and computing courses taught by their faculty rather than mathematics and computer science faculty. These practices, however, were public and as such, were corrected, where necessary, through peer pressure and curriculum committee review. RCM can never be totally self-correcting. Leaders must still both lead and manage.

Enrollment grabbing and hoarding can have a positive effect in RCM. Aware of their enrollment-related revenues, the faculty of Engineering at USC became alarmed at the rate highly qualified engineering freshmen were failing the prerequisite physics courses. They asked, "Why are these bright students failing physics when they are doing well in calculus and introductory engineering courses?" (i.e., and therefore potentially endangering their engineering major). They concluded the problem lay with the physics faculty, rather than the students, and thus challenged their physics colleagues to improve their courses and pedagogy. Since many of the engineering faculty held Ph.D. degrees in physics, the very real threat to teach their own introductory physics classes led to reform in the physics department (whose dean did not want to lose large course revenues!). This story exhibits a positive outcome from knowing the costs of one's actions and who bears them.

- **Schools may offer inappropriate incentives.**

Scott Bice, dean emeritus of the USC Law School, raises the specter of the obverse of trade barriers, namely, the possible "dumbing down" of courses or easing of grading standards to encourage enrollment of students (bringing their tuition revenue) from other departments and schools. His former colleague at USC, Richard Miller (now president of F. W. Olin College of Engineering) offers a similar example within the Engineering School, where a professor of petroleum engineering awarded only As to his students for several years, in an effort to attract more students and to generate more revenue for his department.

"Gut" courses are not a new phenomenon, nor did they arise only because of the financial incentives in RCM. But RCM can certainly exacerbate the problem by adding revenue to popularity! Leadership can and should intervene. Quality control should modulate venality. Or, strategic regulation should modulate laissez faire.

In the early 1980s, when RCM took root at USC, the provost recognized that Letters, Arts and Sciences majors could benefit from access to courses in the very extensive array of professional schools on campus, and encouraged development of general education offerings within such schools as Business, Law, Gerontology, Public Administration, Cinema, Theatre, and the like. The professional school deans saw real revenue opportunities in such courses and proceeded accordingly! The early years of this initiative clearly benefited liberal arts and sciences majors, and the offering schools. But in time, and with a change in provosts, it became apparent that financial incentives were overpowering academic intent. Indeed, some professional schools were focusing too much on their general education offerings, at the expense of attending to the currency and attractiveness of their professional programs. Moreover, the array of general education offerings was making less and less curricular sense even as revenues were being drained from the Letters, Arts and Sciences College.

The thinking that ensued led to clearly reasoned and defined minors in the professional schools, which still had positive revenue incentives, and brought order to the increasingly chaotic general education offerings. The moral: incentives often work, but if left unmanaged, often lead to distortion of academic intent. RCM can never be made leadership-proof.

• **Local optimization may damage the whole.**

As with the issue of trade barriers, it is possible for individual centers to take actions in their own local interest that may not advance the common good. The disorderly proliferation of general education courses just described is a case in point. And there are many others. For example, deans, trying to reduce the indirect costs allocated to their centers to free up revenues for direct program support, may urge reductions in student services, or library costs, or facilities' budgets, even when these costs are necessary to their clients and not unreasonable within the context of their competitive markets. Indeed, those who benefit (e.g., individual students, faculty and staff) rarely have organized budget advocates. Thus, senior leaders have to "hold the center" by speaking up for and funding properly those programs that benefit the whole more than any individual (center) part. This is yet another rationale for revenue taxes to ensure critical central leverage.

A more dramatic example comes again from USC. In the early 1990s, many large private universities across the country experienced dramatic drops in yield, and hence in freshman enrollments. At the same time, financial aid budgets soared. And this experience persisted across several years of entering classes. When confronted with their own tuition revenue losses, several deans of individual schools at USC proposed reducing the quality threshold for admission rather than reducing expenditure budgets. President Steven Sample simply said no. Recognizing that the academic reputation of the university as a whole was at stake, he demanded that quality thresholds be raised and, if necessary, that the university accept a significantly reduced, but better qualified freshman class. Counter to his deans, he saw that reducing revenues and raising quality now were necessary to raising quality and revenues in the future.

While the transition was painful, the outcome has been extraordinary: USC's applicant pool, yields, and academic quality of entering freshmen have skyrocketed. That arguably would not have happened if each dean had optimized his or her revenues. In such instances, central leadership must exert corrective action through persuasion, direct order, or through corrective subvention allocations if available.

• The rich centers get richer.

This complaint usually emanates from a zero-sum mentality, born in centralized budget processes where the revenue pie is owned by provosts and CFOs, and the budget game is maximizing one's own share. The rich may get richer in RCM but not necessarily at others' expense. For example, schools of management have responded well to the "pie-increasing" incentives of RCM while law deans have been particularly persuasive in their arguments to and with provosts (attorneys are, after all, trained negotiators) for subvention. And deans of Arts and Science schools seem preternaturally preoccupied with revenue and cost allocation rules. RCM is a game—entrepreneurs will learn how to play and win by the rules; others will try to play with the rules to win. The real money in RCM comes from proper exercise of the pie-expanding incentives rather than from rearranging rules to claim other centers' money. In the final analysis, institutional leaders have the authority to select center leaders who can be successful, and the responsibility to guide the success of these center leaders through both word and deed.

- **RCM encourages needless argumentation and prevarication.**

To the extent that this attention encourages better, more responsive, and more efficient services, argumentation may not be needless. But the opportunity cost is high: the time spent on changing the rules, thereby redividing the pie, is not available for developing better programs and expanding resources. Here too, the onus is on the leadership to discourage useless bickering. We won't even address prevarication.

- **Public information invites misinterpretation and meddling.**

USC, CGU, and Penn report intervention by trustees in the algorithms for allocating administrative costs and even in the awarding of subvention. This is unfortunate, but it is also the case that trustees have been known to intervene on behalf of specific causes in institutions with other, less public management systems. If there is any saving grace here, at least with RCM, the trustees become involved with the knowledge that the effects of their intervention will be public!

Public information can cause other problems: invidious and unfounded comparison of relative subventions. When people do not understand that a significant component of subvention neutralizes the effects of pairing differential costs of education with common credit-hour prices, for example, they may claim that one center is being ripped-off while another is receiving unearned alms. Comparisons between schools of business and music is a case in point. The claim is almost always wrong. Left alone, without explanation, numbers can mislead. But then, so can a paucity of numbers.

In the early 1990s, when UCLA was beginning to generate RCM budget profiles of the schools, the dean of Medicine believed and proclaimed that the indirect cost recoveries from his school's federal grants and contracts were supporting the school of Letters and Sciences, among others. But when Medicine's indirect costs (facilities and administration) were added to direct expenditures, and the sum compared with Medicine's revenues, there were no revenues left to support anyone else. Moreover, when the impact of large undergraduate enrollments on UCLA's allocations from the state was calculated, Letters and Sciences did not look needy after all. Here, good numbers enabled understanding of the internal economics and purged unfounded, unsubstantiated, and harmful claims. Lore based on no or limited data is no better than misinterpretation of good data! Indeed it's worse since poor data provide no recourse.

We pause to ask, which of the above criticisms are also applicable to the kinds of centralized and relatively decoupled systems RCM was created to change? We think virtually all of them apply, and leave thinking about them one by one as an exercise for the compulsive reader.

Chapter 7

Promise and Performance

In the context of the criticisms just discussed, we now return to the promises of RCM and assess them in greater detail.

- **RCM focuses proper attention on revenue.**

The experience of the University of Pennsylvania (J.C. Strauss, R. Porter, and R. Zemsky, 1979) underscores the importance of resource development. When Responsibility Center Management was introduced in the early 1970s, it was envisioned that deans and department heads would respond to the financial incentives to balance expenditures to revenues by employing intimate local knowledge to effect dramatic changes in expenditure patterns. There were, in fact, dramatic changes, but almost all were focused on using local knowledge to increase revenues, and with significant success. This probably should not have been a surprise. After all, individual faculty operating from their disciplinary departments are one of the bastions of entrepreneurship in our society. Faculty influence enrollment, control content, establish standards and evaluate performance, select and evaluate colleagues, and develop external philanthropic and research support. In an environment that expects responsible financial behavior, faculty have strong incentives and lots of authority to focus on revenue generation. Fortunately, with good leadership, it is relatively straightforward to align these incentives for revenue generation with the furtherance of institutional mission.

These patterns continue today with the Penn deans reporting much greater attention to developing philanthropic and other external revenue by both their faculty and themselves than would be the case in more traditional management systems. The case of USC is instructive here as well. The schools of Dentistry,

Pharmacy, and Urban and Regional Planning literally built themselves on the enrollment and research revenue incentives of RCM. Other schools, like Music, realized that, given unit costs, their further development could not come from enrollment but had to come from gifts and endowments. Coupling of marginal revenues with marginal costs led to appropriately different strategies among the schools.

- **RCM facilitates responsible management of entrepreneurial activities.**

Zemsky and Massy (R. Zemsky and W.F. Massy, 1995) help explain the apparently paradoxical growth of new research institutes at the periphery of many institutions during times of seeming financial constraint. Here, the incentives for external funding have fomented the growth of faculty-centered professional and research activities as add-on or cross-cutting centers to the traditional discipline based departmental structure. This growth at the periphery is not necessarily bad so long as the activities do not detract from the core institutional missions of teaching and research and that these activities pay for their proportionate share of overhead support costs. But with RCM, such growth need not be peripheral at all. Indeed, growth can be absorbed into a standing center, and aligned with the departmental and core institutional missions to provide significant additions of talent, facilities, and resources to the milieu. Responding to revenue opportunities is at the core of RCM, not at the periphery.

The experience of the University of Denver is compelling here. In the late 1980s, Denver's indicators of financial health were pointing and moving in the wrong direction. A new administration diagnosed the core problem succinctly: a disconnect existed between revenue-related decisions in admission, enrollment, and program selection and the level of expenditure authority committed to in the budget. University revenues were not keeping pace with expenditure growth, but the impacts were not immediately visited upon the schools responsible. Denver changed the rules, forcing the coupling of choice with consequences, by implementing RCM. Denver's financial (and academic) health indicators have been pointing strongly upwards ever since, although Craig Woody, Denver's vice-chancellor of financial affairs, reports that several changes in deans along the way were necessary. Lines of business have to be chosen strategically and well when the chooser wins or loses from the choice!

- **RCM aids cost/benefit analyses and trade-off studies.**

In his book (Bill Massy, 1996) on resource allocation, Massy speaks at some length about the resource allocation trade-offs between academic programs requiring subsidy, which he refers to as *intrinsic*, and those which generate additional resources for reallocation elsewhere, which he refers to as *instrumental*. That is a satisfying dichotomy, but it attributes the conventional meaning of the word "intrinsic" to programs that may not deserve it. For present purposes, it is more appropriate to use the less value-laden words: subvened and nonsubvened. A major thrust of RCM, in fact, its original raison d'être, was sensitivity to the marketplace. RCM quantifies the revenues and costs of all programs and demonstrates that the underlying academic or institutional value of a program is independent of whether it is subvened or not. Many programs with high academic value generate net revenue, and some programs with lower academic value require subsidy. For all not-for-profit enterprises, however, after accounting for other sources of revenue, such as general institutional endowment, there must be sufficient excess revenue from nonsubvened programs to cover the subsidies of those other programs of presumably high academic value whose revenues do not cover their costs. Understanding the relative academic value and revenue generating capacities of competing academic programs is facilitated by RCM and absolutely vital to its effective deployment. In truth, it's absolutely vital with any effective management; RCM, however, forces the quantification, and enables the defense.

Sam Preston, dean of the School of Arts and Sciences at Penn, makes this point. He observes that RCM forces deans to determine their most valuable programs on *both* a qualitative *and* financial bottom line basis. If programs are low in quality and high in subsidy, the opportunity costs of protecting a weak academic unit are clear, and the case for change is enhanced. RCM makes cost-benefit calculations possible; central systems tend to legitimate only benefit analysis.

In a 1995 article in *Change*, Bob Zemsky and Bill Massy describe a detailed planning approach Zemsky developed at Penn to quantify academic plans in terms of the number of tenure slots (R. Zemsky and W.F. Massy, 1995). Academic leaders could affect these plans through long-term commitments of subvention. While this approach was logically consistent and made sense from a staff perspective, it failed through either the reluctance or inability of central academic leaders to make and keep the necessary long-term subvention commitments.

By normalizing school and program financial data, physical equivalent measures can be derived from which a number of interesting analyses can be made, both geographically (across schools or departments) and temporally. Tuition equivalent student/salary equivalent faculty ratios or subvention to total revenue ratios by center across time are particularly illuminating. The notion is not that these ratios should be identical across centers. Different teaching methodologies, lifestyles, laboratory needs, revenue opportunities, and histories all contribute to very different measures. The important point is that these measures should be consistent with quality perceptions or expectations, with institutional priorities, and with understandings of relative costs of educational methodologies. If they are not, explicit actions should be taken to realign these measures over time. Organizing data in responsibility center format provides useful, financially consistent management information even if the centers are not being managed on a decentralized basis.

- **RCM provides explicit recognition and support for institutional priorities.**

  The explicit recognition and support for institutional priorities exhibited in RCM budgets encourages good planning and meaningful faculty participation in both the development and realization of those budgets. A number of presidents and provosts, however, have found the discipline of having to make and defend relative priority decisions in public to be very demanding. This issue alone has accounted for the failure of several institutions to realize the full potential of RCM.

  As Jon Strauss described in Chapter 7 of *Resource Allocation in Higher Education* (Massy, 1996), WPI profited from analyses of departmental financial data even though the institution did not employ RCM per se. Many were surprised to find initially that the highest priority engineering departments had equivalent student/faculty ratios some 50 percent greater than those of the more service-oriented science departments. They were even more surprised that one of the flagship graduate programs had an equivalent student/faculty ratio that was less than 20 percent of what had been presumed to be high-priority departments. Subsequently, the common knowledge of this information forced behavioral changes to move those ratios more in line with legitimate expectations.

- **RCM encourages provision of efficient, competitive administrative services.**

In a 1985 *Business Officer* article (J.C. Strauss, 1985), Jon Strauss provides data demonstrating how the relative general institution administrative costs were reduced at both Penn and USC following the introduction of RCM. Detailed studies at USC indicated that school and departmental administration costs were reduced as well. These are clear examples of Meyerson's "marketplace forces" at work. One consequence of charging for administrative costs explicitly is that the resulting costs can be compared to those from alternative providers. Even in those cases where institutional considerations require that the services be provided internally, this comparison is a very powerful motivator for the provision of more efficient services. And, the explicit allocation of certain services, like space related costs, printing, and computing, can actually change usage patterns in the centers.

This argument can be overdone, however. There is the colorful story of a flamboyant dean of Arts and Sciences at Penn suggesting, one hopes somewhat apocryphally, that the best way to balance his budget would be for him to stand on the steps of the library and prevent his students and faculty from entering and thus incurring usage-based charges.

Recent discussions with the provosts and deans at both Penn and USC suggest that neither institution has yet found truly satisfactory ways of assuring that administrative services pass marketplace tests of quality and price. In fact, USC is sufficiently discouraged in this regard that they have fixed the administrative cost allocations to the revenue centers, with guaranteed low annual administration inflation rates going forward, thereby subverting some of the most important incentives in decentralized management: namely, the connections between drivers such as enrollments and research volume, and attendant indirect costs such as student services, library needs, and facilities.

- **RCM yields self-correcting organizations.**

One of the most interesting, yet almost serendipitous, consequences of RCM has been the management improvements that result from the broader participation of faculty and staff in the quantification and implementation of plans they help formulate. This involvement yields a more robust organization that can adapt rapidly to inevitable exogenous changes. This would not be possible without the direct involvement and responsibility of individuals on the front lines, so to speak, who observe the changes first—frequently in their school's revenue statements—and are in the best position to respond creatively. The IUB RCM Review Committee (N. Theobald and M. Thompson, 2000) reinforces this observation in noting, "Primary among these benefits is the ability to address budgetary problems at the level closest to the action, where the information needed to respond to opportunities and cope with problems is most complete." The Total Quality Management movement has emphasized reducing layers of hierarchical management and empowering the individual for exactly the same reason and with the same result.

A 1999 *Change* article describes how one school at USC has adapted the Kaplan and Norton "balanced scorecard" approach to strengthen their case for a larger share of the provost's "academic excellence" subvention (H.F. O'Neil Jr., E.M. Benisom, A. Diamond, and M.R. Moore, 1999). And, IUB's RCM Review Committee (N. Theobald and M. Thompson, 2000) notes: "RCM leads to greater transparencies in budgets. This has allowed the campus to better allocate its scarce resources in a time when the state appropriation plays a declining role..."

Among the most important self-corrections is that enrollment shifts are followed by commensurate tuition revenue shifts. Over recent years, for instance, undergraduate enrollments have shifted dramatically from the hard sciences to computer science across the nation. Under RCM, all else equal, the School of Science would have to cut teaching costs (positions) or argue for more subvention because their revenues were down. The Sciences dean would be forced, as a natural act, to recognize *his* problem. The School of Engineering, on the other hand, would now have the revenues to hire more faculty and add course sections.

In highly centralized universities, such resource reallocations require massive central political will because provosts typically allocate faculty positions, which, once gone, become owned by the deans. Enrollment redistribution is the provost's problem to solve, since she owns all revenues, and the Engineering dean's agony to suffer through. Rarely in centralized systems are resources reallocated even remotely in proportion to changes in student demand. Exercise of too much political will, however, can threaten careers.

Still a different form of self-correction involves general education or distribution course requirements for undergraduates. In many state universities, students and parents in recent years have claimed that insufficient numbers of sections of required courses have delayed graduations, often up to a year or more. IU and the University of Minnesota have both reported that since the advent of RCM, this problem has diminished. Why? Because, like Willy Sutton, departments have recognized that distribution requirements are "where the money is." Crass as it is, the incentive led to the right outcome.

• RCM expresses and quantifies the strategic plan.

All budgeting explicitly or implicitly expresses and quantifies the next years of the enterprise's plan. Unfortunately, it is all too often implicitly, for many organizations' plans are little more than some lofty phrases from their mission statements, and their annual budgets are often simple econometric projections of their prior year budgets, sometimes not even reconciled to actual performance. But, good, bad, or indifferent, these budgets express and quantify plans.

The important distinction of RCM is the explicit requirement to express a relative priority for different institutional activities through that portion of the subvention not devoted to unit price/cost imbalances. This cannot just be relegated to econometric projection. Because subvention is so public and so obviously states relative priority, it focuses careful attention both on the part of the centers in vying for relative favor and on the institutional leadership in dispensing it. The result is a *strategic plan* and the public and participatory character of this process forces a meaningful result. The strategic plans of institutions using RCM may well be couched in the familiar statements of the primacy of the arts and sciences, the importance of undergraduate teaching, and the pursuit of selective excellence. At the core of these plans, however, will be an explicit demonstration of how resources are deployed to achieve these objectives.

• RCM can encourage good academic and administrative outcomes.

Penn (J.C. Strauss, R. Porter, and R. Zemsky, 1979), USC (J.R. Curry, 1996), and Indiana (E.L. Whalen, 1991; N. Theobald and M. Thompson, 2000) have claimed significant academic and administrative improvements as a result of implementing RCM. Fortunately, most would agree that these three institutions all made significant relative gains in their respective peer group rankings following these management changes. There is positive correlation if not causality. These improvements were surely the direct result of good planning and good leadership. But we would also argue that distributed revenue incentives, local entrepreneurship, broad faculty involvement, extensive communication, and explicit priority setting encouraged by RCM structures and information contributed significantly to successful outcomes.

- **RCM helps realize the objectives of collegial governance.**

RCM involves faculty substantively in academic and financial policy with common language and models and formal inputs in the planning process. Alan Wolfe (A. Wolfe, 1996) characterizes faculty governance as a failure and attributes that to a combination of decentralization and tenure. Decentralization and tenure, however, are intrinsic to higher education and Wolfe seems to suggest that, consequently, faculty self-governance is doomed to failure. One of the most promising aspects of RCM has been the establishment of a decision framework with the underlying information on resource deployment and return. With this framework and information, faculty governance can have substantive impact on resource allocation that is conditioned by the normal constraints of both natural limits and the consequences of new revenues and reallocation. Faculty can now move from their all-too-frequent position of dismissible criticism to that of meaningful participation with real data and real responsibility for both success and failure. The differences at Penn, USC, and Indiana in this regard have been remarkable in our judgment.

At Penn, for example, faculty went from general criticism of what they characterized as exploitative indirect cost recovery charges on their sponsored research to genuine understanding of the need to generate revenue to cover the overhead costs associated with the research program. This is not to imply, however, that they wouldn't have liked those charges to be lower! In fact, faculty actually led the movement for indirect cost charges on (private) gift and endowment revenues at Penn to help pay for the associated overhead costs so as to relieve their otherwise inevitable burden on tuition revenue. Further, IUB's RCM Review Committee (N. Theobald and M. Thompson, 2000) indicates, "The RCM process also makes the budget more transparent to all involved and offers an opportunity for responsiveness to the needs of students and faculty."

- **RCM focuses attention on cost control, price restraint, and educational outcomes.**

The higher education literature of recent years has been rife with the need to place greater emphasis on learning, to reduce price escalation if not prices themselves, and to limit growth of administration, plant, and student services. And, society is demonstrating increasing impatience at the obvious reluctance, if not inability, of the educational enterprise to address these issues with the vigor and the results already demonstrated by American industry, in general, and health care in particular, at least until recently. Decentralized management provides a vehicle for evaluating these reform issues and establishing quantifiable plans to address them, as such plans should not be just well-meaning statements in commencement speeches and annual reports. By the very nature of RCM, these plans have to be expressed in explicit pricing, expenditure authorizations, and resource reallocations, the consequences of which can be observed and measured by all of the institutional constituents. When subventions are *properly* parsed and understood, one can also infer cross-disciplinary subsidies and the fact that several, if not most, instructional programs cost more than the tuitions they charge.

Chapter 8

Lessons Learned

Here are the lessons we have taken away from our experiences, observations, and interviews.

- **You cannot make RCM perfect by continually refining the algorithms and the rules.**

  We have met and lived with academic and administrative officers who believe that perfection is only a rule change away, and every localized issue can be handled by a systemic change. Those who pursue this path are doomed to replicate the Internal Revenue Service. Some rule changes do, indeed, improve structured incentives. But too much drives out entrepreneurship and leaves little time for focus on academic direction. Bear "keep it simple" in mind. Keep Gresham in mind.

- **Entrepreneurial systems do not necessarily create entrepreneurs.**

  Too many years of perfecting pie division turn off the pie-expanding gene. Congenital entrepreneurs will take to the RCM incentives. But provosts may have to change their deans to match entrepreneurial capability with the system's incentives.

- **Subventions are *not* self-correcting.**

  As Michael Masch, budget director at Penn, points out, subventions can ossify. If they become entitlements through lack of frequent refreshing and renewing of their rationales, then the president and provost can lose their abilities to affect the direction of the whole. Which is to say, the whole defaults to the sum of the parts. Holding and advancing the commons requires active and aggressive leaders.

- **Subventions are not welfare.**

Leaders need to remember and document the parts which comprise subvention—so much for neutralizing the cost/price mismatch; so much for plan success; so much for advancing institutionwide goals; so much for promising startup ventures.

- **Central service providers need incentives to be efficient.**

This issue is typically overlooked in RCM, but as long as deans have to balance their expenditures to the dual constraints of their revenues and the indirect costs "handed" to them, central services can act like monopolies and stiff their customers. Sometimes the stick is the better incentive than the carrot; central administrative services providers need to know that they can be outsourced, and occasionally they should be, if only to make a point. Then these providers will learn that they have to know their competitors' service prices, meet or better them, or at least demonstrate greater local knowledge and better services, to earn the business of the deans. Services cost back-pressure from the responsibility (revenue) centers appears not to be enough. The University of Denver has successfully used benchmarks and balanced scorecard assessments to controls costs and improve services in conjunction with decanal pushback.

- **Provosts and chief administrative officers need to measure and manage administrative services and costs in *both* central units and responsibility centers.**

We have seen many instances of deans of centers, flush with revenues and unhappy with central services, hiring their own administrators to supplement services they are already paying for in their allocated indirect costs. In some cases, where there is a unique clientele needing focused attention, this is warranted. In other cases, it is symptomatic of an unresponsive central administration, where failure to recognize and correct a service problem denies economies of scale, and shifts costs to the deans who invoke local solutions.

Engaging the issues and managing the balance are imperative. Sometimes, central service units need a budget champion to enable them to scale services to meet increased demand—even if the indirect costs allocated to and paid by the revenue generating centers increase materially!

- **Talk about RCM's rules and incentives can consume all the time available.**

This is seductive stuff for smart people. Some talk about the rules and incentives is useful and can lead to productive structural changes. But a monomaniacal focus on rules is doomed: it is ultimately all seduction and no consummation. Qualitative, academic talk has to become the strong currency, by dent of leadership. Otherwise, Gresham's law obtains.

- **RCM presidents and provosts need sufficient and liquid subvention resources.**

If the subvention pool begins to evaporate, or if subventions become politically hardened, (i.e., become de facto entitlements), then the critical ability to steer the whole is lost. Presidents and provosts need to contribute to the growth of subvention sources by raising unrestricted gifts (for consumption or endowment) and by guarding against importunities from deans to restrict internal resources available for general use.

- **RCM deans need professional financial officers.**

In centralized budget systems, managing a direct expenditure budget is relatively easy. But managing a responsibility center budget requires comprehensive understanding of the center's business model: to predict and budget the center's tuition revenues, one must understand the external student recruitment market and the internal course enrollment patterns; to predict and budget indirect cost recovery on center contracts and grants, one must know the indirect cost rate and predict the center's (modified) total direct expenditures to plan and manage the annual budget; to manage *total* expenditures, one must master the indirect cost allocation rules and the responsibility center/central service interface. Typically, smart amateurs who have grown from administrative assistants into local budget managers won't be good enough. And while professionals cost more, they find resources for their deans.

- **RCM presidents and provosts need surge tanks.**

Under some circumstances, revenues can redistribute among centers more rapidly than their expenditures budgets can accommodate. Transitional subvention allocations can help smooth the redistributions—if they are available. This lesson is clearly related to its predecessor. Stable environments facilitate good education.

- **RCM requires strong central leaders willing to defend quantitative expression of relative priorities.**

    The many times that the need for a different kind of leadership under RCM has been mentioned should be some indication of its importance. All too many leaders of the past have cloaked their actions in secrecy and intrigue, hoping to convince each program and center that they were among the most favored. This seldom works. And, like the old story about the requirements for being a good liar (not that any direct parallel is being drawn consciously), the secretive approach to leadership requires a very good memory. RCM requires that leaders build bases of informed support for explicit and very public bets on the future. This is a very different approach, but it is very much in keeping with the traditions and strengths of collegial governance, and it can be very effective. Moreover, the deans and other center leaders under RCM must lead, not just "administer."

- **RCM needs a resident intellectual champion.**

    RCM is a structure designed to balance academic entrepreneurship with fiscal responsibility. The end game is responsible academic growth and development. RCM needs rules. They are means to the end game.

    People not raised in RCM and who inherit leadership roles in RCM universities are often captivated and captured by the rules and the legions of faculty who would change them. The rules then become the end game, and like the Tax Code, become ever more elaborate. Then winning is defined by litigation to effect pie redistribution. Entrepreneurship is driven out, and institutions can stagnate. Intellectual champions never lose sight of the true end game, and force academic focus and rule simplification to keep lawyers and accountants from governing the academy.

Chapter 9

Conclusions

The history and current state of RCM confirm, in part, the early claims of efficiency and effectiveness. But the criticisms and lessons learned make very clear that formal decentralized management requires never-ending vigilance to assure that the fundamental incentives are not being subverted, and a major commitment from institutional leaders to work within and appropriately adapt the system. RCM works best with strong deans *and* strong provosts, CFOs, and presidents. Dynamic tension is necessary to match the will of the parts with the way of the whole.

We acknowledge a positive bias towards RCM, having committed so much time and effort to its conception and evolution. We know something about life before and after. RCM is, by far, not perfect. But one should ask, compared to what? We know of no university that, having fully implemented RCM, has gone back, although we know of two which made a run at RCM and stopped short of unleashing the inherent incentives and responsibilities. Once RCM is in place, people get addicted to the information connecting all the moving parts! Devolution into the black box is not an option.

RCM is a response to centralized budgeting, characterized by provosts and CFOs dispensing massive numbers of small favors (e.g., faculty slots, secretarial positions, information system resources, physical space) through a black box process. In the old model, authority is local (residing in departments, labs and schools), responsibility is central, and the two are out of balance, with all the problems that can create. We said this at the outset. Most readers will recognize this state of affairs, and can judge for themselves whether RCM is a better option.

Bibliography

Curry, J.R., "Budgeting," *College and University Business Administration*, Sixth Edition, Washington, D.C. : National Association of College and University Business Officers, 2000.

Curry, J.R., Chapter 7 in *Resource Allocation in Higher Education*, Ann Arbor: The University of Michigan Press, 1996.

Chabotar, K.J., "Managing Participative Budgeting in Higher Education," *Change*, Vol. 27, No. 5, (September/October 1995).

Keohane, N.O., "Becoming Nimble, Overcoming Inertia," *Harvard Magazine*, (January–February 2001).

Massy, W.F., *Resource Allocation in Higher Education*, Ann Arbor: The University of Michigan Press, 1996.

O'Neil Jr., H.F., E.M. Benisom, M.A. Diamond, and MR. Moore, "Designing and Implementing an Academic Scorecard," *Change*, Vol. 31, No. 6, (November/December 1999).

Salamon, L.B. and J.C. Strauss, "Using Financial Incentives in Academic Planning and Management," *NACUBO Business Officer*, (November 1979).

Strauss, J.C., R. Porter, and R. Zemsky, "Modeling and Planning at the University of Pennsylvania," *Financial Planning Models, EDUCOM*, (1979).

Strauss, J.C., "Indirect Cost Rate Reduction Through Management Action," *NACUBO Business Officer*, (November 1985).

Theobald, Neil and Maynard Thompson, Co-chairs, RCM Review Committee, 1999-2000, "Responsibility Centered Management at Indiana University Bloomington," (May 2000).

Wolfe, A., "The Feudal Culture of the Postmodern University," *The Wilson Quarterly*, Vol. XX, No. 1 (Winter 1996).

Whalen, E.L., *Responsibility Center Budgeting*, Bloomington: Indiana University Press, 1991.

Zemsky, R., Editor, "A Call to Meeting," *Policy Perspectives*, Vol. 4, No. 4 (February 1993).

Zemsky, R. and W.F. Massy, "Expanding Perimeters, Melting Cores, and Sticky Functions: Toward an Understanding of Current Predicaments," *Change*, Vol. 27, No. 6 (November/December 1995).